THE SILENT
MERVILLE
BATTERY
A POCKET GUIDE

The 9th Parachute Battalion's Crucial D-Day Assault

The purpose of this book is to enhance the experience of visiting the Merville Battery by taking you on a tour around the site, explaining what happened and where during the 9th Parachute Battalion's assault in the early hours of D-Day.

- **A comprehensive guide and short walking tour**
  - **Explains what happened and where**
  - **Features original wartime photographs**

Neil Barber

Copyright © 2019 Neil Barber.
All rights reserved. No part of this publication may be reproduced, stored in a retrieval system, or transmitted, in any form, or by any means, electronic, mechanical, photocopying, recording or otherwise, without the prior permission of the publisher and copyright holder, nor be otherwise circulated in any form of binding or cover other than that in which it is published and without a similar condition including this condition being imposed on the subsequent purchaser.

Neil Barber has asserted the moral right to be identified as the author of this work.
Designed and typeset by Ian Bayley.
British Library Cataloguing in Publication Data
A catalogue record for this book is available from the British Library
Published by Sabrestorm Publishing, The Olive Branch, Caen Hill, Devizes, Wiltshire SN10 1RB United Kingdom.

Website: www.sabrestorm.com
Email: books@sabrestorm.com

ISBN 978-1-78122-013-9

Whilst every effort has been made to contact all copyright holders, the sources of some pictures that may be used are obscure. The authors will be glad to make good in future editions any error or omissions brought to their attention. The publication of any quotes or illustrations on which clearance has not been given is unintentional.

THE SILENCING OF THE MERVILLE BATTERY

A POCKET GUIDE

- A comprehensive guide and short walking tour
- Explains what happened and where
- Features original wartime photographs

Neil Barber

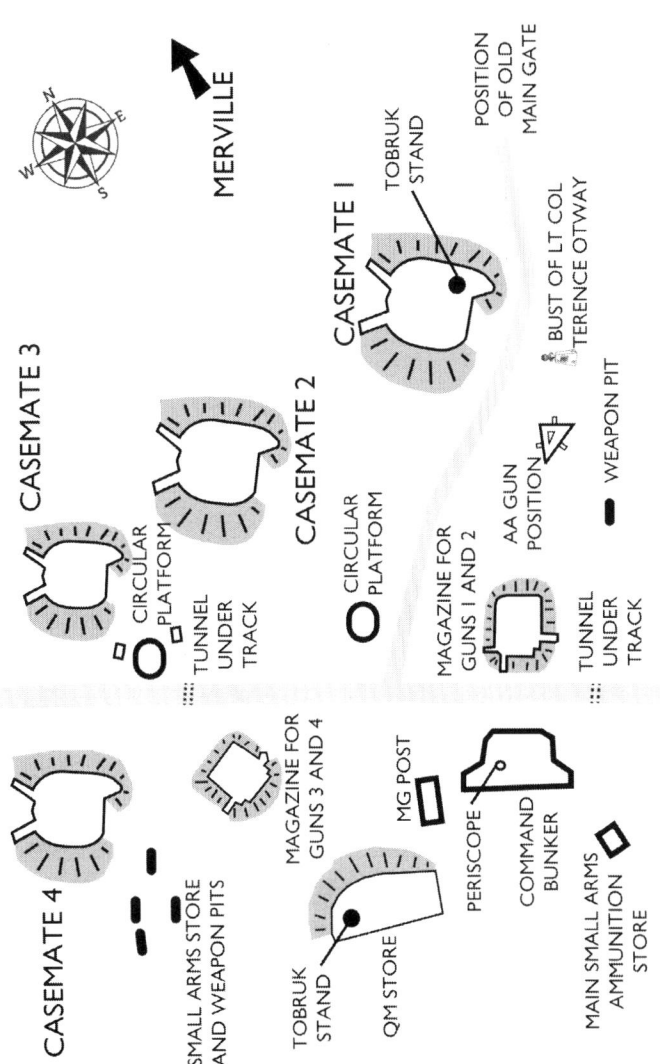

Contents
Following the guide

Introduction	6
The Merville Battery - The Background	7
The Plan to Silence the Battery	14
D-Day - Tuesday 6 June –	
The Bombing Raid	20
The Drop	20
The Reconnaissance	24
The Assault	28
Aftermath	50
The Casemates	51
Further Reading	52

Following the guide

Although this guide provides an in-depth explanation of the 9th Parachute Battalion's D-Day assault on the Merville Battery, it has been specially written to be used while walking around the site. It details various positions where the relevant explanations can be digested and pondered, providing a better appreciation of the efforts of the parachutists.

Introduction

With seventy five years having passed since D-Day and the eventual success of Operation Overlord, we tend to forget that with so many differing Services and tasks involved, plus of course, very capable and determined German forces in wait, the chances of failure were immense.

Of all the problems to surmount, the first was the breaching of the defences of Adolf Hitler's much-vaunted 'Atlantic Wall'. The Merville Gun Battery was a part of that Wall.

> **The Merville Battery was the last resting**
>
> **place for many brave men.**
>
> **As you walk around the site,**
>
> **please keep this thought in mind.**
>
> **This is hallowed ground.**
>
>

The Merville Battery
The Background

There had been a German artillery presence as a fixed position on the Merville site since the summer of 1941. Underground ammunition bunkers and the large circular platforms that can be seen were built to provide a more stable platform for the guns to fire in any direction, but the main purpose of the Battery was the protection of the entrance to the vital Caen Canal, 3km to the west.

As the strategic situation gradually changed in the West, the German High Command decided that the guns required protection from bombing, and so by December 1942 the construction of the first and largest of the four casemates, Number 1 was underway. With the guns being of indirect fire nature, meaning that the target could not be directly observed, it was also necessary to build a Forward Observation Point on the coast. The purpose of the Battery remained unchanged, so the gun casemates actually point towards Ouistreham.

By 1944, the possibility of an Allied invasion of Europe had become only a matter of time. The Anglo-American planners knew that the most critical

Casemate 1 under construction

period for the landings was the early stages, when unhindered time was needed to get ashore, establish the beachhead and then build up men and materiel. Consequently, intelligence gathering had intensified, and the defences, including the construction of all gun emplacements along the occupied coastline, were closely monitored.

With the decision for the invasion to take place in Normandy, the Merville Battery's location became of paramount importance as it had the ability to fire along the length of the proposed SWORD Beach, just beyond Ouistreham, and so it was imperative that the Battery be silenced before the landings began.

The background of the Merville Battery

Reconnaissance aircraft began to photograph the progress of the Merville Battery constructions, and it was estimated from the casemate size that they would contain guns of up to 150mm calibre. Attempts were made by RAF Bomber Command to destroy the site, but with the casemate walls being in places up to two metres thick and covered

An aerial reconnaissance photo showing the four casemates and other buildings marked by the photographic interpreter

The Silencing of the Merville Battery

with earth, they proved to be almost impervious to bombs. Such bombing did hinder the building work, but the Merville Battery gradually came into being.

The Battery photographed on 30 May 1944, after several bombing raids. Note the unfinished anti-tank ditch to the left

The Battery's defences were formidable. Two belts of barbed wire surrounded the site, the inner being a fearsome two metres high by three metres deep. Between these belts was a minefield, while other mines had been sown in various approach routes around the perimeter. A 365-metre anti-tank ditch, five metres wide by three metres deep, wound its way around the west and north-western sides. One hundred and twenty soldiers manned the defences, which included many machine-gun positions and a 20mm Flak 38 anti-aircraft gun.

To highlight its importance, during late May 1944, various high-ranking Wehrmacht officers inspected the Battery, the first being Generalleutnant Erich Marcks, commander of 84 Korps. His next visit was as part of a group led by the Commander of the 7th Army, Generaloberst Friedrich Dollman. However, the most illustrious visitor was General-Feldmarschall Erwin Rommel, Commander of Army Group B (7th and 15th Armies), who inspected the site on two occasions, the last being on 27 May.

On the night of 19 May the commander of the Battery, Hauptmann Karl-Heinrich Wolter was killed during a bombing raid while in the old Mairie, on the edge of the perimeter, close to the main entrance.

Field Marshal Erwin Rommel visiting the Merville Battery

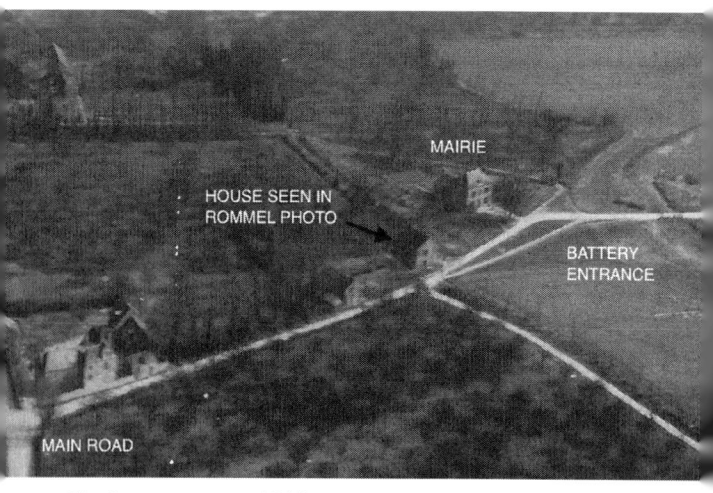

The Battery entrance 1944

The following day a junior officer, Leutnant Raimund Steiner, was put in temporary command until a more senior officer became available. However, it was he who met Rommel on his final visit, and Steiner was still in command on 6 June.

Lt Raimund Steiner

The plan to silence the Battery

Airborne Forces, in the shape of the British 6th Airborne Division, were to seize the area east of the River Orne and act as a defensive buffer for the eastern flank of the invasion. This gave the Division many important tasks for D-Day, but its initial primary objectives were the capture, intact, of the bridges over the Caen Canal and the River Orne at Benouville, the demolition of five bridges in the Dives area to the east and the silencing of the Merville Battery. The Merville task was assigned to Lieutenant Colonel Terence Otway's 9th Parachute Battalion.

Officers of the 9th Parachute Battalion, April 1944

The battalion was to land on Dropping Zone (DZ) 'V', two kilometres east of Merville. Beforehand, the DZ was to be secured by 'C' Company of the 1st Canadian Parachute Battalion, jumping at 0020 hours, while Pathfinders of the 22nd Independent Parachute Company began setting up the navigational aids for the main drop which would begin at 0050 hours.

Two advance parties of the 9th Battalion were to drop with these early arrivals; an RV Party to set up the Rendezvous and organise the DZ for the arrival of the battalion, and a Reconnaissance (Recce) Party to reconnoitre the Battery, meet the battalion outside the objective, advise Colonel Otway on the prospects of the plan, and lead the unit to the Battery perimeter.

Between 0030 and 0050 hours, approximately 100 heavy bombers were to 'soften up' the objective.

After the battalion's main drop, a Taping Party was to assemble and head straight for the Battery. Using mine detectors, they were to clear three gaps in the minefields up to the main perimeter fence, and mark these lanes with tapes.

DZ 'V' at Varaville to the Merville Battery

The bulk of the battalion was to assemble on the DZ along with various units attached specifically for the assault, these being a section of the 4th Airlanding Anti-Tank Battery Royal Artillery with six-pounder guns, to blast open the steel doors of the casemates (if required) and Royal Engineers of 591 (Antrim) Parachute Squadron to actually destroy the guns. Transport gliders would bring in the anti-tank guns along with the Engineer's specialist explosives and other heavy equipment such as jeeps, pneumatic drills and ladders. Heavy casualties were anticipated, and so Number 3 Section of 224 Field (Parachute) Ambulance was to set up a dressing station along the road on the eastern side of the perimeter.

The Assault Plan

The whole group would leave the DZ for the Battery at 0235 hours. After meeting the Recce Party in Gonneville-sur-Merville, just to the east, the relevant information would be passed on, the plan confirmed, and the assault would begin. A Diversion Party was to move around to the main gate and create as much noise as possible, while two sniping groups picked off various designated targets.

THE MERVILLE BATTERY ASSAULT PLAN

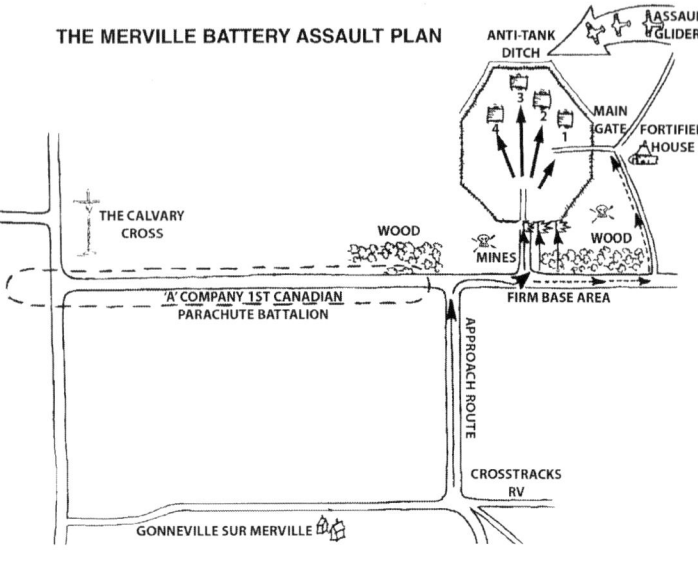

'B' Company men were to crawl through the mine-free lanes and slide Bangalore torpedoes beneath the wire. However, before detonating them they had to wait for three Horsa gliders carrying men of 'A' Company (plus several further engineers and explosive charges) to land within the Battery itself. When the gliders were down, the Bangalores would be detonated and four 'C' Company assault groups would charge through the gaps in the wire, each heading for a designated casemate. The assault was set for 0430 hours.

Following the completion of the assault and the destruction of the guns, Royal Navy signallers jumping with the 9th Battalion were to contact HMS Arethusa, a warship lying off the coast, to relay the success message. If Arethusa did not receive this or any other signal, she was to open fire shortly after 0500 hours. The battalion was therefore on a tight schedule to complete the action and get clear of the site.

The Paras had trained over many months for this task and each man knew his exact rôle in the assault. They could not have been better prepared.

> If you are visiting the Battery, the ideal viewing position to read the next section is close to the bust of Lieutenant Colonel Otway.

D-Day
Tuesday 6 June

At around 0015 hours, things began to happen in the area. The sound of low flying aircraft could be heard overhead and to the east, beyond the main road. It was the arrival of the 6th Airborne Division's *Coup de Main* party for the capture of the Caen Canal and River Orne Bridges, Pathfinders and the advance parties of the various battalions.

The bombing raid

Ten minutes later, a sound could be heard that grew in power as it became louder and louder. It was the formation of 100 heavy bombers. The raid on the Battery itself began. There were explosions all around, but few bombs fell on the Battery itself. Unfortunately, just across the main road, the small village of Gonneville-sur-Merville suffered heavily.

The main drop

Twenty minutes later, at 0050 hours, thirty Dakotas carrying over 600 men of the 9th Parachute Battalion, approached the Normandy coast. Ahead of them was a huge dust cloud resulting from the bombing raid. This, plus the effect of flak, some

D-Day - Tuesday 6 June

turbulence and a fifty kilometre per hour wind buffeting the planes, caused many pilots to take evasive action. This resulted in chaos amongst the Paras as they prepared to jump because many were thrown to the floor. To compound matters for the pilots, several of the devices to identify the DZ, set up by the Pathfinders, had been damaged in the drop and were not working.

Consequently, the Paras were scattered over a wide area, many of them landing in a region that had been flooded by the Germans just to the east of the Varaville DZ. One of them was Private Ron Tucker:

I could see a small track below and luckily for me I landed on it. As soon as I got out of my parachute I heard the sound of boots running towards me. There was a small hedge about four feet high and I jumped over that and got as near underneath it as I could. I held my breath and listened to the soldiers talking and examining the 'chute. There were three of them. I pulled out the pin of a '36' grenade. If they wanted me I was at least going to take a few of them with me. Another soldier arrived on a bike, obviously an officer because he gave an order and they began to search for me, peering over the hedge. One of them stood so close to my face that I could smell the dubbin on his boots. It couldn't have been long but it seemed like ages, when suddenly the officer gave another order and they ran off down the road. I put the pin back in the grenade, removed my rifle from its protective sleeve and went off down the road in the opposite direction.

The Battalion had been so widely spread that two hours later, 0250 hours, the latest appointed time to leave the RV, only 150 men had arrived. There was also no sign of their transport gliders carrying the heavy equipment and so there were neither anti-tank guns to employ nor explosive charges for the Engineers to silence the guns. There were no Navy signallers nor signalling equipment, no mine detectors, no Field Ambulance surgeons and only six medical orderlies with their First Aid kit. Only ten lengths of Bangalore torpedo and a solitary Vickers medium machine gun had been recovered. No mortars had been found, which meant there was nothing with which to illuminate the Battery for the three assault gliders. Finally, no contact had been made with 'A' Company of the Canadian Parachute Battalion, which was to cover the left flank during the assault. However, in spite of this nightmare scenario, Colonel Otway decided that there was no choice but to continue with the mission. He did still have 150 highly trained, determined men.

Lt Col Terence Otway

While Otway's men made their way towards Gonneville-sur-Merville, Major Smith's small Reconnaissance Party was beginning its task at the Battery.

> The ideal viewing position for the following explanation is on top of no 2 casemate, looking east, towards the main road.

The Silencing of the Merville Battery

The Reconnaissance

Major Smith's three-man Recce Party comprised himself and Company Sergeant Majors 'Dusty' Miller and Bill Harrold.

Using the photo below, you are now standing on the casemate that is 2nd from the left. Looking east, towards the main road, the area was strewn with bomb craters. As you can see, a small wood used to run from the track on the right, along the length of the road. Smith and Miller cut the cattle fence wire just inside the corner of the wood where it met the track. Miller kept near its edge, close to the track, while Smith moved sideways, so that they were about 30 metres apart. This was

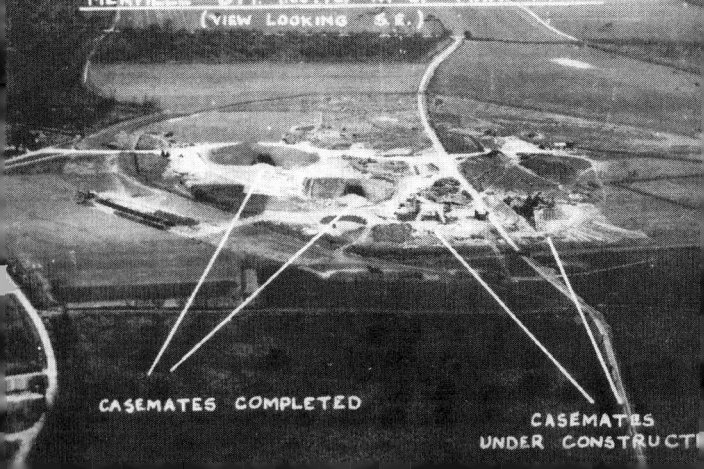

to avoid the possibility of them both being killed if a mine exploded. On their hands and knees, they began to crawl through the wood and approach the Battery. They encountered a number of wires that were attached to mines, and these were either cut or passed over. On reaching the inner edge of the wood, they cut their separate gaps in the wire of another cattle fence, and moved into the open ground, which was covered in long coarse grass about 30cm high. They crawled towards the outer wire of the Battery, 100 metres beyond the concrete wreckage (which was the position of a 20mm flak gun) to the right of Colonel Otway's bust. There they listened for five minutes, heard nothing and then crawled towards one another. They then decided to move 150 metres along the wire in both directions, Miller going to the right and Smith to the left, towards the main entrance. They confirmed that south of the track (or to the right as you look at it), there were two belts of barbed wire separated by a 30-metre gap, while north of the track there was only one belt of barbed wire. Therefore, this would definitely be where they would blow gaps in the wire.

Miller was sent back with this information. No sound at all had been heard from within the Battery and Major Smith began to wonder if it was actually occupied. He therefore began to crawl through the single belt of wire, but even on its own, this was a formidable obstacle:

The wire was about five feet high and fifteen feet wide. It seemed to be made to no particular pattern, but was thick with many supporting stakes. Cautiously I began to push various strands of wire aside and hook them back. Crawling half on my side and half on my back, I crept carefully into the hole I was making. My body was not more than half under the wire when I thought I heard a click, a familiar noise often made by a fidgety sentry knocking his rifle. I listened and heard it again probably within thirty yards. At crawling level there was a small rise hiding the ground in the direction of the noise from my view. I could not be certain of its origin and decided to carry on. I felt it imperative for me to be certain whether or not the Battery was held, and if so more about its ground defences. I continued my crawl.

It was slow and tedious work. Even on a dark night, if the head is held low, the wire can be seen against the sky. Twisting loops back and fastening them down was a simple but slow job. The main

trouble was the numerous pieces which seemed to pop up from nowhere and catch on the rest of the body after the head and shoulders had passed.

He was about halfway through the wire when suddenly there were excited voices over towards the main entrance. He looked in that direction and saw a tug aircraft and glider come into view, flying at about eight hundred feet. This immediately brought the Battery to life, and there was shouting from everywhere, voices booming out orders, these being relayed and acknowledged. Four machine guns opened fire with tracer but the glider and tug came straight on, passing right over the centre of the Battery. The 20mm flak gun also opened up, firing rounds with red tracer. The whole scene lit up the Battery. Noting the positions of the anti-aircraft weapons, as soon as the firing stopped, Smith began his own withdrawal and returned to Gonneville where he met Captain Paul Greenway and part of his Taping Party. They had a huge problem with none of their mine detectors or tape having been found on the DZ. Paths through the minefield still had to be cleared. CSM Miller led the party to the Battery where he, Greenway and two men commenced to clear four lanes through the minefield by searching for them with their bare hands and marking the route by dragging their feet to scratch lines in the earth. Two men were left on the edge of the wood at the 'entrances' to these lanes.

The Assault

The journey to Gonneville took the 150 parachutists around an hour and a half. Colonel Otway duly met Major Smith (a plaque now commemorates this at the crossroads) and reported on his reconnaissance and the efforts of the Taping Party.

A new plan was rapidly formed. Only two gaps were to be made in the main wire. Four assault groups, each reduced to around fifteen men, would then head for a casemate. The Officer Commanding the Assault Company ('C'), Major Ian Dyer, and his second in command, Captain 'Robbie' Robinson were both missing, and so the Colonel gave Major Allen Parry the responsibility for organising the

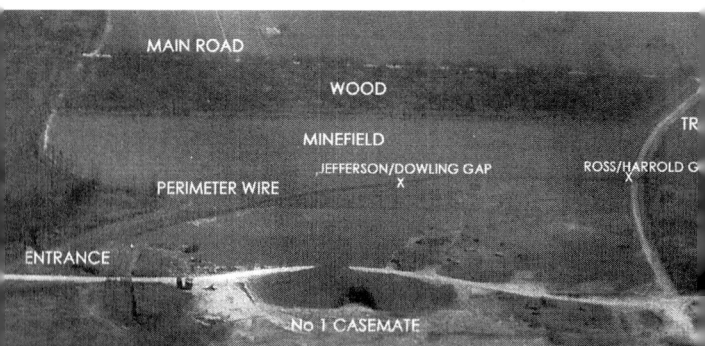

D-Day - Tuesday 6 June

assault groups. Parry hastily assigned four commanders. Lieutenant Alan Jefferson would lead the No 1 casemate group, Lieutenant Mike Dowling No 2 group, Company Sergeant Major Barney Ross No 3 group and Colour-Sergeant Harold Long No 4 group. Major Parry would follow with an 'A' Company party behind those heading towards No 1 casemate.

Maj Allen Parry

Major Smith led the 150 men up the track from Gonneville. As they reached the road and turned right to begin the move towards the wood, two German heavy machine guns opened fire. These were immediately dealt with, one by the small Diversion Party heading for the main entrance, and the other by the men operating the solitary Vickers machine gun.

The Diversion Party, led by Sergeant Sid Knight, then began to approach the Battery along the track over to your left, at the edge of the field, around the Battery perimeter and began firing towards the entrance, while on the main road, the men had

THE MERVILLE BATTERY ASSAULT

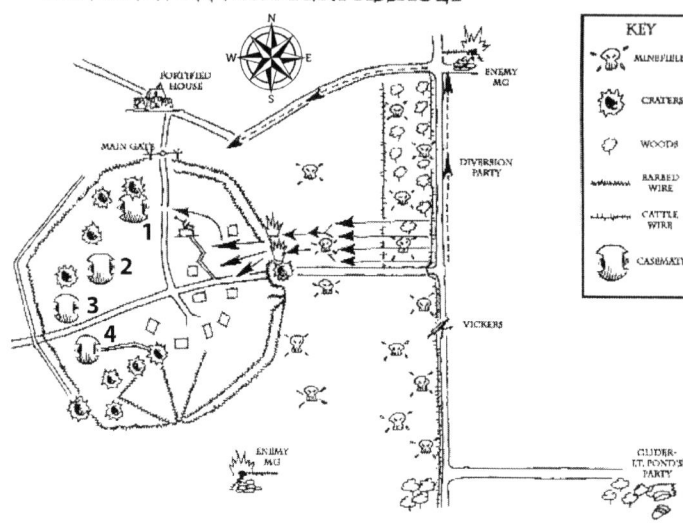

begun to move into the wood via the four cleared paths. Major Smith:

The Breaching Parties followed in single file after the guides from the Taping Party. They disappeared into the darkness carrying their few Bangalore torpedoes, and were closely followed by the Assault Parties.

One of the gap positions was very close to the track on the right (running through the Battery), while the other was almost directly in front, being around 100 metres in from the track. The 'B' Company men pushed their scaffold pole-like Bangalore torpedoes beneath the wire, which again was 100 metres beyond the concrete wreckage to the right of Colonel Otway's bust. They then withdrew a short distance.

Behind them, the assault groups filtered into the lanes, some taking up position among the bomb craters at the 'start line' about fifty yards from the belt of barbed wire. They readied themselves for the signal to move and awaited the arrival of the three Horsa gliders carrying the 'A' Company assault party. With nothing to illuminate the Battery, the pilots just had to make their best attempt.

> The recommended place to read the following is to the right of the wreckage of the concrete flak gun position.

The Silencing of the Merville Battery

The assault groups did not have to wait long, as a Horsa appeared overhead and was immediately engaged by anti-aircraft fire from outside the Battery. It circled the area four times but could not locate the Battery and continued off to the east. Shortly after, another glider came in at a very low altitude. This time the anti-aircraft gun opened fire, letting loose, according to Lieutenant Jefferson, "*bursts of five rounds that appeared like glowing, red balls.*" The third burst hit the glider, which began to smoulder as it passed directly above No 1 casemate, carried on over the wood and landed close to the track up which the Battalion had advanced from Gonneville. (Trees line the lower end of the track and identify the area where the glider landed. See map page 30).

Upon exiting, these troops stopped a German patrol that was heading towards the Battery and therefore the landing position turned out to be very fortuitous.

Sgt Sid Knight

Lt Paul Greenway

CSM 'Dusty' Miller

With no sign of the final glider, they could wait no longer. A whistle was blown and the Bangalore torpedoes detonated, creating the two gaps in the wire. With support fire blazing away, the assault groups of Jefferson and Dowling headed for the gap directly in front, while those of Ross and Long went for that near the track. Frank Delsignore was heading for No 1 casemate:

Alan [Jefferson] was the first one up on his feet and led us into the assault. Any fear I had was gone. We were up and running with Alan, firing from the hip as we went in. We knew there were land mines in the ground we had to cover.

To spur his men on Lieutenant Jefferson was blowing a toy hunting horn.

The Germans reacted quickly. Flares were sent up into the sky and fire rapidly increased from various positions around the site. Booby traps and mines were going off and the defenders began to concentrate their fire waist-high on the gaps in the wire. Another of Jefferson's men was Sid Capon:

I remember shouts from the left saying "Mines!,

mines!", and explosions. We carried on zig-zagging, running the gauntlet of the crossfire.

Alan Jefferson fell to the ground close to the anti-aircraft gun platform, suffering wounds to the legs. Fierce hand-to-hand fighting began as the Paras forged their way towards the casemates.

There were a number of deep craters between the men and the casemates, some over 15 metres wide. Fred Milward was a member of Major Parry's group:

With shouts and cries and a few curses as well, we charged after Major Parry over the minefield, through the gap blown in the wire and straight for the guns just as fast as we could. I found myself spending half the time running up and down bomb craters. There were so many bomb craters overlapping one another and it was all loose earth…. If you ran down in one, you had a hell of a job getting up the other side. It was like trying to climb up a sand dune, everything was moving. I saw Major Parry go down and several of my pals hit as they charged forward.

D-Day - Tuesday 6 June

Major Allen Parry:

I was conscious of something striking my left thigh, my leg collapsed under me and I fell into a huge bomb crater. I saw my batman [Private George Adsett] *who was just alongside me, looking at me as if to say, "Bad luck mate", and off he went.*

With more distance, and therefore wire, craters, trenches and enemy positions to negotiate, it was perhaps an even tougher proposition for those men heading for Numbers 3 and 4 casemates.

CSM Barney Ross:

The longer you was out there, the longer the bloody bullets and shit were flying about !

CSM Barney Ross

In the darkness and smoke, the Colonel could not see how his men were faring, so he moved forward with his Reserve group, to the gap in the wire used by Jefferson's platoon. This enabled him to observe both left and right:

35

I had to be able for example, looking to my right to see Sergeant Knight and whether they'd managed to get in through the gate. Equally, I had to be in the best position from the machine gun on the left of the position. In addition, I had to keep on dodging this sod, a machine gun up on the tower, who was shooting at me. So I was moving in and out.

Sergeant Knight's Diversion party had gradually worked its way forward to deal with the machine guns near the main gate.

With the firing and explosions continuing unabated, Otway decided to send in the remainder of his force:

Like many men, I suppose, I had no great fear of being killed but the horror of being mutilated swept over me when the moment came to go through the wire into the enemy fire. Quite irrelevantly, I wondered what Wilson [his batman] would think of me. I shouted, "Come on!" and ran for it. In the circumstances it was the only thing to do.

They headed through the gap. In various places some of the men had to fall on what was left of the wire while the others ran across their backs.

D-Day - Tuesday 6 June

Major Bestley:

Terence Otway ordered me to sort out a machine gun half-left of the axis of assault. The rest of my Company being committed to the gap they had blown, I set off with my batman in the direction indicated. I had not gone more than fifty to a hundred yards when a bullet clipped a nerve behind my left knee, incapacitating me.

Maj Harold Bestley

Beside Otway was his adjutant, Captain 'Hal' Hudson:

I was just short of the gap in the wire when something hit my right buttock. I assumed it was a piece of earth, or a stone thrown up by mortar or shell fire. I was extremely surprised to find myself thrown on my back and assumed that some sort of blast must be responsible. However, on attempting to get to my feet, I found that I was

Captain 'Hal Hudson

unable to do so. I put my hand on my right buttock and was very surprised indeed to find it smothered in blood. I felt no pain, but a curious weakness. Lying on my back, looking towards the Battery through the gap in the wire made by the Bangalore torpedoes, I saw a stream of machine-gun tracer which appeared to be uninterrupted. Through this gap were pouring the assault troops.

I could see German troops outside the gun emplacements, presumably others were in the casements. With infinite pains I took up my revolver, aimed carefully at the nearest German, and pulled the trigger. Unfortunately, the bullet went straight through my left foot. This self-inflicted wound caused me the most exquisite pain.

Hudson did not realize how badly he had been wounded and was more concerned about his foot. Otway himself was very fortunate when one bullet hit his water bottle and another went through the back of his smock.

The first men to reach the rear of a casemate were those going for No 1, the closest.
Sid Capon:

D-Day - Tuesday 6 June

There were four of us, Eric Bedford was now the senior NCO, and there was Frank Delsignore, 'Johnnie' Walker and myself.... It suddenly seemed all quiet. We lobbed two grenades in there and all of a sudden heard movement inside. In the left-hand compartment, the Germans started pushing each other out and lined up opposite. I wasn't worried about the gun, I wasn't worried about anything, only the Germans. The last one wore glasses and I think he thought he was going to be shot.

Sid Capon

Ken Walker was a signaller within HQ Company:

We were told that our job was to wipe out the German machine-gun posts which were inside the Battery between No 2 and No 3 casemates – most of them were Schmeissers in pits... There were two Germans with

Ken Walker

a machine gun, and myself and another soldier ran towards it, and as we ran towards it they upped and ran away. I fired my rifle and missed, did it again and I'd had all my ten shots, and I wasn't aware of firing them.

Only about four of CSM Ross' party survived to reach No 3 casemate:

The door was shut. It was a long way round to the front of the bloody things…, turning round the corner and shooting bullets into the eyelets. We were milling around the top. We were poking some grenades down the air vents. By the time we'd done this on the top, the door was then coming open and they were coming out.

CSM Jack Harries had made it to No 4 casemate:

I moved to the entrance of the gun emplacement but there was plenty of activity inside with bodies milling around like a crowded railway carriage. Germans were running out of the exit and being picked off as they went.

D-Day - Tuesday 6 June

Barney Ross:

I think there were a lot of Polish guys amongst them, all shouting "Comrade, comrade", with all their bloody hands up.

The enemy evacuated the casemate and the Paras went in expecting to find the 150mm gun, only to be confronted by a wheeled 100mm Field Howitzer on a platform. Following up, Sergeant Fred Dorkins of 'A' Company also reached No 4 and entered the casemate:

Fred Dorkins

There was CSM Jack Harries, another man and myself. We decided to elevate the gun. Damaged the elevating gear and placed a Gammon bomb on the breech block with a short fuse. It seemed to work, causing considerable damage.

CSM Jack Harries

Gradually, resistance around the site began to weaken. It had almost petered out when another machine gun opened fire from a building near the entrance, outside the perimeter. Sergeant Knight immediately marched some prisoners straight towards the machine gun. At that, the gunner stopped firing and surrendered. This signalled the last of the fighting within the Battery.

The resulting scene was appalling. Len Daniels stated that the whole area pervaded a peculiar odour of freshly turned earth, smoke, cordite and torn flesh, a smell the survivors would never forget. Dead and wounded of both sides lay everywhere and the Paras began to help them as best they could, but with the shortage of doctors and medics it was an impossible task.

Len Daniels

Worryingly for the survivors, apart from some yellow signal flares, there was no method of contacting HMS Arethusa, which was due to shell the Battery, and

Lieutenant Jimmy Loring

D-Day - Tuesday 6 June

so they had to leave the site as quickly as possible. Lieutenant Jimmy Loring did have a carrier pigeon, The Duke of Normandy, which he released from its container.

The Duke of Normandy

The recommended place to read the following is outside No 1 casemate.

In the other three casemates, attempts were being made to put the guns out of action using various means, but with no Engineers or specialist explosive, their options were limited.
Major Parry:

In the bottom of my rather personal bomb crater, I assessed my position. My left leg was numb and my trouser leg was soaked in blood. Having a minuscule knowledge of first aid I

43

removed my whistle lanyard and tied it to my leg as a tourniquet. My knowledge was evidently too limited, as I applied it in the wrong place. Realizing, after a brief interval, my error, I removed it, thus restoring some form of life to my leg; sufficient at any rate, to enable me to clamber out of my hole and continue with my appointed mission.

He managed to hobble to the entrance of No 1 casemate, where he saw a few Paras attending to the wounded, but there was no sign of his batman, George Adsett. The group of German prisoners was still stood there with their hands in the air:

Most of them were wearing greatcoats and soft hats and didn't appear to be expecting us. As I entered the enormous casemate it was possible to discern only two or three of my party. I was somewhat weakened by the loss of blood and passed through the casemate to the firing aperture at the far end, where, to my intense dismay, I saw not a 150mm gun, as was expected, but a tiny, old-fashioned piece mounted on a carriage with wooden wheels... , it was clearly a temporary expedient pending the arrival of the permanent armament. This was an awful anti-climax, and made me wonder if our journey had really been necessary.

He sat for a moment on the sill at the bottom of the firing aperture and as he did so, there was an explosion immediately outside and he felt something strike his wrist. Fearing that he had lost his hand, he was relieved to see that it was only a small gash from a shell splinter. He proceeded to deal with the gun:

We all carried sticks of plastic explosive, detonators and fuse wire and I instructed a sergeant to make up a suitable charge which was placed in the breech of the gun.

Private Bill Picton:

A chap named Vic Simpson and myself were given the job of spiking the German gun which we did with Gammon bombs.

Fred Milward:

We set up the explosive

Fred Milward

and then we were ordered outside and I curled up beside a wall. There was an enormous bang and smoke came curling out of the doorways.

Major Parry:

We re-entered the casemate, now full of acrid smoke, and upon inspecting the gun I was reasonably satisfied that sufficient damage had been inflicted upon it to prevent it playing a part in the seaborne assault, which was due in two and a half hours.

> The recommended place to read the following is outside No 4 casemate.

Privates George Hawkins and Alan Mower of 'B' Company had gone in as part of the Reserve Force. On reaching No 4 casemate Mower left his few companions outside, went in to investigate and found the field gun, unaware of what had been done previously to the gun. He only possessed two '36'

Alan Mower

fragmentation grenades, and so decided he could either put them in the wheels to try and bring the gun down, or throw them in with the ammunition. He went back outside to inform the others of his options, but did not get the chance:

There was this explosion and we sort of fell in a heap together. I fell on the Bren gunner and it was obvious he was dead. Hawkins and me were just riddled with shrapnel. It caught me in the back, legs, arms and went through into the wall of my chest.

George Hawkins:

The boy on my left got it all in the face…. And I suppose the other boy behind, shrapnel came up and went right through his head, killed him outright. I just laid there. It just knocks you silly.

George Hawkins

The Germans had begun shelling from a gun battery further along the coast. The Paras were ordered to evacuate the site and so the seriously wounded were hurriedly dragged out or placed in casemates.

Sergeant Len Daniels:

It was just a shambles virtually, coming out of the Battery and making your way back. Like people coming out of a football match. We didn't march out, we came out in a bedraggled line. Didn't exactly form up as such, the thing was we were so close to the knuckle that we'd got to get out as quickly as possible. There was one or two people going "Come on, get on, get out quick". We got out, and all followed along.... You met one, "Is that you Joe ?", "Is that you Fred ?" That sort of thing as you went along.

The Rendezvous was a Calvary at a crossroads 700 metres to the south (which can still be seen). Private Ken Walker, HQ Company:

Here for the first time, I realized some of the horrors of war, never having been in battle before. I was absolutely exhausted and feeling depressed as if suffering from the after effects of an attack of influenza. Most of the soldiers appeared to be in the same state, which could also be described as total bewilderment.

Major Parry, who could no longer walk, found a trolley just outside the Battery and made his way to the Calvary on this.

Major Smith witnessed his arrival:

He took a brandy flask from his pocket, gulped a mouthful and beamed, "A jolly good battle, what ?" The grim faces of the men burst into smiles, and the sullen group of prisoners looked on in bewildered amazement. He insisted on being allowed to stay with the Battalion, but the Commanding Officer ordered him to go to the Regimental Aid Post and he did so reluctantly.

Len Daniels:

Wandered up and down finding out what's what and who's there, and trying to organize bits and pieces, and that's when I saw the Colonel sitting on the Calvary, with his head in his hands. He had been through a tremendous amount. To take what few men he had in to attack that Battery was beyond human expectancy.

Sergeant Knight carried out a head count and found only seventy-five men still standing. However, their sacrifice was not to be in vain. The guns were silent when the first waves of Allied troops landed on SWORD Beach, and by the evening of D-Day, the bridgehead there had been duly established. The bravery and sacrifice of the men of the 9th Parachute Battalion saved many lives on this momentous day.

Aftermath

Due to the mistaken belief that SWORD Beach was being shelled by the Battery, No 3 Commando was ordered to attack it on 7th June. However, again they did not have the correct explosives to permanently destroy the guns. They suffered heavy casualties while pulling out.

The Merville Battery remained in Germans hands until August and continued to fire whenever a target presented itself, but this usually invited a torrent of fire from Allied warships.

Leutnant Steiner commanded the Battery throughout the battle of Normandy and during the withdrawal of the German Army from Normandy, the 'Ruckmarsch' eastwards. The Battery was actually evacuated at 0200 hours on the 18 August, and later that day the Belgian Piron Brigade, under the command of the 6th Airlanding Brigade, advanced into Merville. The 2nd Oxf and Bucks occupied the area of the Battery and used No 1 casemate as a headquarters. During the subsequent weeks the Germans were pushed back through France, and Steiner and one gun crew were eventually captured by Allied Forces in Ypres on the 6 September.

The Casemates

No 1 casemate has been returned to a similar layout to when it was occupied by the Germans on the 5 June 1944. The sight and sound display provides a vivid impression of being inside a casemate during the early hours of D-Day.

No 2 casemate is a shrine to the 9th Parachute Battalion, a place to sit and reflect, and to see the faces of those who actually took part in the operation.

No 3 casemate explains the actions of the Commandos in the area. The 1st Special Service Brigade was under the command of the 6th Airborne Division.

No 4 casemate details the actions of the 6th Airlanding Brigade in Operation Paddle, the plan for the clearance of the enemy up to the River Seine. It also explains the actions of the 2nd Oxf and Bucks, the 12th Devons, the Dutch Princess Irene Brigade and the Belgian Piron Brigade.

Further Reading

If you are interested in finding out further detail about the actions of the 9th Parachute Battalion at the Merville Battery and in the surrounding area during the following week, The Day the Devils Dropped In by Neil Barber is available in both paperback, Kindle and E-book.

Also available -
'Pegasus Bridge – A Pocket Guide'.